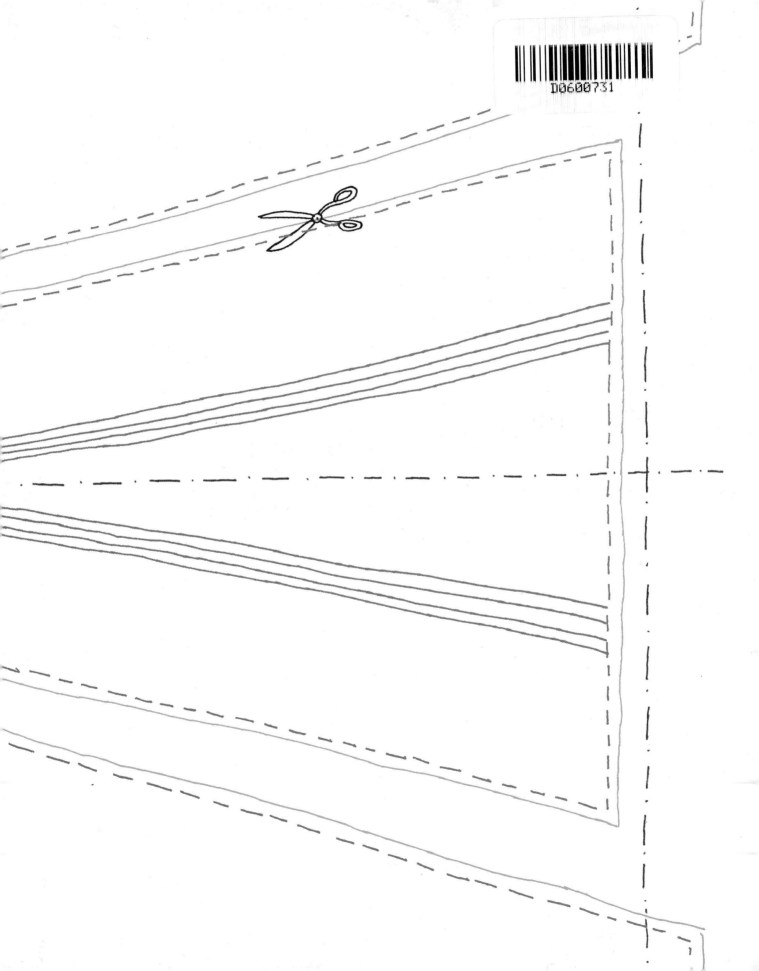

Annemarie van Haeringen was born in the Netherlands. She is a
Dutch illustrator and picture book author and illustrator. She studied art at
the Rietveld Academy in Amsterdam. Annemarie has illustrated numerous
children's books, worked on a series of films, and created illustrations for
several children's magazines.

She won the Golden Brush Award three times—in 1999, 2000, and
2005—and a silver for *Coco and the Little Black Dress* in 2014. This is her
first book with NorthSouth.

First published in the United States, Great Britain, Canada, Australia, and New Zealand in 2015
by NorthSouth Books, Inc., an imprint of NordSüd Verlag AG, CH-8005 Zürich, Switzerland.

Distributed in the United States by NorthSouth Books, Inc., New York 10016.
Library of Congress Cataloging-in-Publication Data is available.
ISBN: 978-0-7358-4239-7 (trade edition)
1 3 5 7 9 . 10 8 6 4 2
Printed in China by Leo Paper Products Ltd., Heshan, Guangdong, April 2015.
www.northsouth.com

FSC
www.fsc.org
MIX
Paper from
responsible sources
FSC® C020056

ANNEMARIE VAN HAERINGEN

COCO

AND THE
LITTLE BLACK DRESS

North
South

"HURRY UP! You're not going to bed until all the sheets are ironed!"

Coco sighed. She lived in an orphanage even though her father was still alive. It was worse than being an orphan: she felt rejected, abandoned, as if she were a mistake . . . a little nothing. Coco was very tired, and she was always hungry. She felt as fragile as an eggshell.

"Coco! Pay attention! Pull that thread out and follow the pattern, NOW!"

Coco dreamily looked outside at the barren garden with nothing but empty flower beds and black ponds. Ponds as black as the big dresses the "aunties" wore.

Sometimes she was allowed to stroll, preferably when the sun was shining so she could smell summer — and for a brief moment no laundry soap.

By age eleven Coco was very good at sewing. She also knitted, crocheted, mended, embroidered, and repaired stockings. She worked very, very hard.

Everybody knew that the girls from the orphanage could embroider like angels.

When Coco was a young woman, she found a small job as a seamstress. In the evenings she danced and sang in a nightclub. She never wanted to be poor again. But if she wished to become rich and famous, she would need to do more.

She made wealthy friends, and stayed in their houses, entertaining them with her singing. It was very different than the convent.

The homes were dignified and stately. Everywhere she looked there were beautiful colored carpets and doors with copper knobs.

Squires and baronesses came to visit with their genteel ladies and friends. They threw lavish parties and hunts.

Ah! thought Coco, watching as if she saw the wind change direction. *So this is what rich people do! They go to parties, to the races, and to the beach. But look at their clothes . . . those hats! How can you think with a dead pigeon on your head?*

"Pull harder, I say! Tighter! I need a figure like a wasp."
Those corsets! Coco watched in astonishment at the way the dignified ladies laced themselves up — so tight they sometimes fainted. *They look elegant, though. They can even mount a horse like that. Riding sidesaddle—with two legs on one side.*

When you're horseback riding, you belong to their world. That's what
Coco wanted. But not in a skirt! Riding was difficult enough as it was.

"Can I borrow your jodhpurs?" she asked the stable hand one day.
She held up the trousers to see how they were designed.

Then she sewed a pair for herself. "Now I need a quick study in staying on top of a horse — while walking and at a full gallop."

"Watch Coco," the ladies said. "Look how she sits on her horse."

Sit? thought Coco. She bounced on her horse like a Ping-Pong ball!

But Coco persevered. Soon she drew attention wearing her jodhpurs and was invited to ride with the men.

She also got invited to the races. "But you have to wear a hat!"

Coco bought two dozen straw boater hats from a thrift store and decorated them herself.

"Oooh!" all the ladies called. "Ah! We want a cute hat like that too! No fruit baskets on our heads anymore!"

There were enough genteel ladies to start a hat shop. And that is what Coco did.

She created other things too. . . .

"I'll never wear a corset!" said Coco. "Nor endless skirts with full hips. I'll make a dress that you won't even feel when you're wearing. A dress you can dance in and ride a bicycle with."

Coco made loosely fitted knit dresses and cardigans. With pockets, just like the ones men wear.

Coco looked like a cute doll. Everybody agreed.

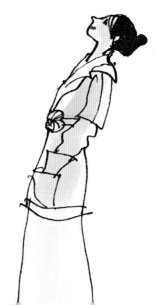

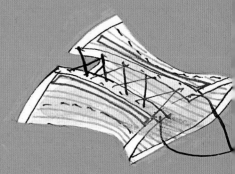

The dignified ladies, glorious in their full skirts and tightly laced corsets, watched jealously.

"What beautiful clothes! So fine, so ultrafine." "So supple, like running water in a river." "We want that too! Away with corsets!" "Did you see that?" "I saw it first!"

The ladies flocked to Coco's shop to indulge—dresses like a second skin, travel coats to live in, hats that could be folded in a suitcase—easy, luxurious, and chic. And the icing on the cake: Coco's perfume. A perfume that smelled like a beautiful woman.